ADORABLE ANIMAL BABIES

# BABY ANIMALS IN THE RAINFOREST

SARAH RIDLEY

PowerKiDS press

Published in 2026
by The Rosen Publishing Group, Inc.
2544 Clinton Street, Buffalo, NY 14224

First published in Great Britain in 2021
by Wayland



**Editor:** Nicola Edwards
**Designer:** Lisa Peacock

**Cataloging-in-Publication Data**

Names: Ridley, Sarah.
Title: Baby animals in the rainforest / Sarah Ridley.
Description: Buffalo, NY : PowerKids Press, 2026. | Series: Adorable animal babies | Includes glossary and index.
Identifiers: ISBN 9781499453584 (pbk.) | ISBN 9781499453591 (library bound) | ISBN 9781499453607 (ebook)
Subjects: LCSH: Rain forest animals--Juvenile literature. | Rain forest animals--Infancy--Juvenile literature. | Rain forest animals--Ecology--Juvenile literature.
Classification: LCC QL112.R535 2026 | DDC 591.734--dc23



Manufactured in the United States of America

CPSIA Compliance Information: Batch #CSPK26. For further information contact Rosen Publishing at 1-800-237-9932.



Picture acknowledgements:

Dreamstime: Feathercollector 24, 29br; Deborah Hewitt 16b; Grant Phillips 17t, 17b,29tl. Nature PL: Oriol Alamany 10; Adrian Davies 8t; Suzi Eszterhas 12, 15t; Michael & Patricia Fogden/Minden 21b, 26; Doug Gimesy 22b; Nick Hawkins 5b; Mark Moffett 20; Anup Shah 6; Dave Watts 25t, 25b, 29bl. Shutterstock: Lucas Barros 5t; BorneoRimbawan 8b, 28bl; Claire E Carter 11t; Davehuntphotography 2,14r, 29tr; Dirk Ercken 18c; Nico Faramaz 23b, 28tl, 32b; Steffen Foerster 21t; Rachel E Foster 16t; GTW 4b; Andrey Gudkov 9b; Hajakely 13t; Imagebroker 14l; iPics 11b; LMspencer front cover, 28br; Manamana title page, 4t; Mazur Travel 7; Jeroen Mikkers 18b,19t; Paleokastritsa 23t; Martin Pelanek 22t; Pfotenpaparazzi 11c; Rikrik 19b, 28tr; Miguel Schmitter 13b; Seanoneillphoto 27b; Thorsten Spoerlein 27t; Lillian Tveit 9t; Juan Francisco Valbuena 15b.

# CONTENTS

Rainforest Babies 4
Orangutan Babies 6
Mountain Gorilla Babies 10
Ring-Tailed Lemur Babies 12
Cairns Birdwing Caterpillars 16
Strawberry Poison Dart Frog Tadpoles 18
Flying Fox Pups 22
Rainforest Chicks 24
Can You Remember? 28
Glossary 30
Answers 31
Index 32

Words in **bold** are in the glossary on pages 30-31.

# RAINFOREST BABIES

**Rainforests** are full of life! The warm, wet weather makes plants grow all year round. They provide food and homes for animals and their young.

High in a rainforest of Central America, a sloth cares for her baby.

In the Amazon rainforest, capybara families live near rivers and **wetlands**.

In a tree in Brazil, this golden lion tamarin is raising twins.

On the forest floor in Central America, a tapir and her **calf** search for plants to eat.

# ORANGUTAN BABIES

Orangutans live in **Borneo** and **Sumatra.** Every evening, a mother orangutan and her baby rest in a new **nest** she made from leaves and branches.

For the first two years, the baby goes everywhere with its mother. It will drink her milk for six years.

The mother plays with her baby! The games are fun and help the baby grow stronger.

The baby learns how to cling to branches with its hands and feet.

The mother shows her baby which fruit, nuts, leaves, and insects are good to eat. Slowly, the young orangutan learns a **food map** of the forest.

Mother and baby travel through the forest together for about eight years, until it's time for the mother to get **pregnant** again.

# MOUNTAIN GORILLA BABIES

Mountain gorillas live in the rainforests of Rwanda, Uganda, and the Democratic Republic of the Congo. Mother gorillas hug, feed, and care for their babies.

Mother and baby stay close to each other for the first four years.

A baby gorilla clings to its mother's back as she moves around the forest.

Slowly babies learn from their mother which plants are good to eat.

Mothers and their babies live in **family groups**. They rest close to each other during the day and snuggle up at night.

# RING-TAILED LEMUR BABIES

Ring-tailed lemurs live in the rainforests of Madagascar. These babies are two weeks old.

A lemur baby drinks milk from its mother for the first five months. The mother *purrs* at her baby and the baby *purrs* back.

The lemurs live in a group called a troop. They call to each other with *howls, clicks,* and *barks.*

After about a month, baby lemurs start to explore and play with other lemurs. They always stay close to their mother.

The mother wraps her tail around her baby to make it feel extra safe.

Lemurs **groom** each other, and each other's babies. This removes **pests** and builds strong **bonds** between lemurs in the troop.

Soon the baby will be able to leap through the trees or run along the ground like the adults in the troop. At five-months-old, baby lemurs can find food for themselves.

# CAIRNS BIRDWING CATERPILLARS

The female Cairns birdwing butterfly is the biggest butterfly in Australia. She has a clever way of making sure more of her babies survive.

Mating butterflies

After she has **mated** with a male, she lays her **eggs** on a poisonous plant.

When they **hatch**, the **caterpillars** munch on the leaves of the plant. Birds know not to eat them because the poison from the plant collects in the spines on the caterpillars' backs.

When they are ready, the caterpillars change into butterflies. This male butterfly has just pulled itself out of its **chrysalis**.

# STRAWBERRY POISON DART FROG TADPOLES

Strawberry poison dart frogs live in the rainforests of countries including Brazil and Costa Rica. Unlike most frogs, these frogs care for their young.

The female finds a mate by following the noise of his calls. They mate and she lays about six eggs.

Night and day, the father protects the eggs. He keeps them damp by peeing on them!

When the **tadpoles** hatch, the mother carries each tadpole high into the treetops where **bromeliad** plants grow.

She climbs down into the center of a bromeliad where a pool of water collects. The tadpole will slide down into its new home.

Then the mother collects the next tadpole until each one is in its own plant pool.

Now begins a daily trip to each of the plant pools where the mother left her tadpoles. She lays **unfertilized** eggs for them to eat.

Over the next six to eight weeks, the tadpoles grow and change into **froglets** and then frogs.

# FLYING FOX PUPS

Flying foxes are also called fruit bats as they eat fruit, **pollen,** and **nectar**. These gray-headed flying foxes are resting in the treetops of rainforests in Australia.

After it is born, a flying fox **pup** clings to its mother's fur, drinking her milk, and staying safe.

When the mother flies off to find food, her pup goes with her.

After four or five weeks, the mother will leave her pup hanging next to other pups while she goes in search of food. When she returns, mother and pup cuddle up again.

The mother and pup stay close until the pup is about six months old.

# RAINFOREST CHICKS

Rainforests around the world are home to thousands of different kinds of bird and their **chicks**.

High in the treetops in Central America, a pair of harpy eagles built this nest. Together, they will bring monkeys, sloths, and birds to feed their chick.

In an Australian rainforest the male cassowary cares for the young. After the female has laid her eggs on the forest floor, he keeps them warm for the next 50 days.

When his chicks hatch, he leads them around the rainforest, showing them what is good to eat. His chicks call to him *peep, peep* and he calls back. The family stays together for about nine months.

The stripe-tailed hummingbird lives in the rainforests of Central America. She built the nest, laid the eggs, and kept them warm. Now she will feed the chicks until they are ready to leave the nest.

In a rainforest in South America, scarlet macaws raise their chicks together in a tree hole. Both parents feed their chicks for up to two years.

In the Amazon rainforest, the family group helps to care for young hoatzin chicks. They feed the chicks leaf soup.

# CAN YOU REMEMBER?

Now that you have read about some rainforest babies, can you remember their special names?

1.

2.

3.

4.

5.

6.

7.

8.

The answers are on page 31.

# GLOSSARY

**bond** strong feelings between animals

**Borneo** a large island in southeast Asia, shared between Malaysia, Indonesia, and Brunei

**bromeliad** a plant that attaches itself to a rainforest tree branch. Water collects in the center of its leaves to form a pool.

**calf** a baby tapir or other baby animal

**caterpillar** the stage in a butterfly or moth's life cycle, after it has hatched from an egg

**chick** a baby bird

**chrysalis** the stage in a butterfly or moth's life cycle when it changes from a caterpillar into an adult inside a protective covering

**egg** a rounded object produced inside the body of a female animal. If it is fertilized, a young animal will develop from this egg.

**family group** parents, their adult offspring, and young

**food map** a memory map of where food can be found, and when it is ripe

**froglet** a tiny frog that will grow into an adult frog

**groom** to clean an animal's fur

**hatch** to come out of an egg

**mate** when a male and female animal join together to have babies. A mate is also the name for the partner of an animal.

**nectar** sweet liquid made inside the flowers of plants

**nest** a place built by animals in which they keep their eggs or young safe

**pest** an annoying animal that lives in the fur of other animals, or harms plants or homes

**pollen** a fine dust produced by the male part of flowers

**pregnant** when a baby is developing inside an animal

**pup** the name for the young of many types of animal, including bats

**rainforest** a thick forest where it rains a lot

**Sumatra** a large island in Indonesia

**tadpole** the young of a frog, toad, or newt

**unfertilized** when an egg has not joined with a sperm to make a new living thing

**wetlands** swamps, marshes, and other areas of land where the soil is covered by, or full of, water

Answers

1. flying fox pup; 2. strawberry poison-dart frog tadpole; 3. orangutan baby; 4. mountain gorilla baby; 5. Cairns birdwing caterpillar; 6. ring-tailed lemur babies; 7. cassowary chicks; 8. harpy eagle chick.

# INDEX


bats 22–23, 28
birds 24–27, 29
bromeliads 19–20
butterflies, Cairns birdwing 16–17

calves 5
capybaras 4
caterpillars 16–17, 29
chicks 24–27, 29

eggs 16, 18–19, 21, 25–26

foxes, flying 22–23, 28
frogs, strawberry poison-dart 18–21, 28

gorillas, mountain 10–11, 28

lemurs, ring-tailed 12–15, 29

orangutans 6–9, 28

plants 4–6, 8–9, 11, 15–17, 19–22, 24, 27
pups 22–23, 28

sloths 4, 24

tadpoles 18–21, 28
tamarins, golden lion 5
tapirs 5